S0-BRT-697

 6/ex

Books by the same author

Four Seasons West, a photographic odyssey of the three prairie
provinces. Printed 1975. Reprinted 1980
Grant MacEwan: No Ordinary Man, a biography. Printed 1979.

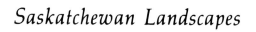

Saskatchewan Landscapes

Saskatchewan Landscapes

by Rusty Macdonald

Western Producer Prairie Books, Saskatoon, Saskatchewan 1980

Copyright © 1980 by R. H. Macdonald
Western Producer Prairie Books
Saskatoon, Saskatchewan

Printed in Canada by
Modern Press ⬤1
Saskatoon, Saskatchewan

Design by Ray Statham
Photo Editor: Doris Macdonald
Cover Photograph location: Marquis, Saskatchewan

Western Producer Prairie Books publications are produced and manufactured in
the middle of western Canada by a unique publishing venture owned by a group
of prairie farmers who are members of Saskatchewan Wheat Pool. Our first book
in 1954 was a reprint of a serial originally carried in *The Western Producer,* a
weekly newspaper serving western Canadian farmers since 1923. We continue the
tradition of providing enjoyable and informative reading for all Canadians.

Canadian Cataloguing in Publication Data

Macdonald, R. H., 1915-
    Saskatchewan landscapes

    ISBN 0-88833-054-5

    1. Saskatchewan - Description and travel -
1950-   - Views.* 2. Saskatchewan - Quotations,
maxims, etc. I. Title.
FC3517.3.M24   917.124'0022'2   C80-091033-8
F1071.M24

Dedication to the Homesteaders

Pushing the frontiers further
    Back with relentless hands,
Blazing the trail with a plowshare
    Far in the hinterlands;
Holding fast to their birthright,
    Born to the realm of toil;
Bearded, grim and unconquered,
    Ragged kings of the soil.

Building their lonely cabins,
    Staking their homestead claim;
Beating the trail to Somewhere,
    Steady, fearless and game,
Bounded by sky and muskeg,
    Hedged by the vast unknown,
Earning their hundred and sixty,
    Winning their fight alone.

Theirs is the dream eternal,
    Hills that are rugged and green;
Lure of the far horizon,
    Prairies, wind-swept and clean,
Visioning towns in the making
    Faith in the untried lands,
Holding the country's future,
    Safe in their calloused hands.

from The Best of Edna Jaques

Contents

Acknowledgment

The author is indebted to many persons and institutions called upon during the production of this work. To name them all would inevitably result in omissions. However, constant use was made of the Saskatoon Public Library Information Centre and Saskatoon History Room, as it was, to a lesser extent of the Shortt Historical Library at the University of Saskatchewan.

Attention is called to the list of authors, poets and publishers which begins on page 87 at the back of this book, for they are the ones who were generous enough to permit use of quotations from their works published in a number of books for the completion of this book. We are grateful to them for their help. This work would have been impossible without the Photo Editor, Doris Macdonald who knew the collection better than the photographer and where and what everything was.

The Author

Introduction

The content of this book owes its origin to the courageous men, women and children who, filled with hope, faith and courage, and ignoring the seeming impossibility of the task, broke the tough turf and sowed the seed which made possible a community that grew into the broad rich Province of Saskatchewan. They came from many countries and spoke many languages but were united in their objective which was to find freedom and opportunity in which to grow.

Few of the landscapes that appear in the following pages were taken without seeing in them somewhere the ghostly figures of pioneers who made it all possible. They had neither the riches nor the leisure in which to carve their names on stone but, unwittingly, they carved them in western soil which has proven to be a far more durable monument to their achievements than bronze, stone or steel. Study the landscapes closely for, although unseen, their presence is felt in all that surrounds us. These are the ones we celebrate in our anniversaries.

Much has been written over the years about the land of their choice. Early writers dealt with it as with the unfamiliar, the great unknown, and so drew a sombre picture. In his monograph *Far Horizons, Man Alone**, dealing with landscape and man in Saskatchewan writing, Carlyle King states:

> *"The pervasive image in serious writing about the Saskatchewan scene has been one of lonely distance. The prairie is extensive, empty, quiet — and unconcerned."*

Among the earliest writers was William F. Butler who reconnoitered the prairie region from October 1870 to February 1871. Whether it was due to the fact that he had missed the fly season or not, Captain Butler enjoyed what he saw but, unfortunately for the early reputation of the prairies, he chose as title for the book he later wrote, *The Great Lone Land*.

Stating that certain French writers had described the prairie region as terrible and oppressive, Captain Butler disagreed with them:

> "But for my part the prairies had nothing terrible in their aspect, nothing oppressive in their loneliness. One saw here the world as it had taken shape and form from the hands of the Creator. Nor did the scene look less beautiful because nature alone tilled the earth, and the unaided sun brought forth flowers . . . A glorious country to ride over — a country in which the eye ranged across miles and miles of fair-lying hill and long-stretching valley; a silent beautiful land . . . upon which summer had stamped so many traces that December had so far been powerless to efface their beauty."

These were not the words of a detractor and yet, as has been the fate of other similar reports, the title was enough for most people and the impression that the western part of Canada was a place to be avoided became implanted firmly in the public mind, without further reading of his book.

As Dr. King's words suggest, writers who came after Captain Butler did little to dispel the dismal reputation whether they wrote poetry, fiction or non-fiction. However, there were others who were to see the brighter aspect of Saskatchewan's varied and rolling landscape, usually to be found among more recent writers. Possibly this is due to the fact that life on the prairies is now kinder, with the wilderness conquered, much of the endless toil reduced by men, machines and technique, and the isolation removed by roads, cars, aircraft, telephones, railways, radio and television. Whatever the reason, growing numbers of authors are recording their reactions to the positive attributes of the region and, in this way, replacing the old with a new reputation in the public mind.

It was among the latter group of works a search was made for quotations to match scenes captured by the camera to be included

2

in this book. It was an eerie experience for, just as the photographer saw the pioneer in his mind's eye in many of the landscapes, so certain passages in poetry and prose seemed to suddenly conjure up the figure of the writer. It seemed that gaps of time and distance were bridged and that all three became involved in the operation in some mysterious way.

That is what this volume sets out to do, to bring all three together: the pioneer, the writer, the beauty of Saskatchewan. To the extent that it succeeds in doing so, it may earn the privilege of a place among the many who remember and celebrate the achievements of those who have gone before.

R.H.M., Saskatoon 1980

*Far Horizons, Man Alone; Landscape and Man in Saskatchewan Writing by Carlyle King, a Mary Donaldson Memorial Lecture delivered in Saskatoon Public Library auditorium May 12, 1973, and sponsored by Saskatchewan Library Association. Printed by Western Producer Book Service 1974 (now Western Producer Prairie Books).

Saskatchewan Prairie

Here was the least common denominator of nature, the
skeleton requirements simply, of land and sky —
Saskatchewan Prairie.

W. O. Mitchell

The River

The Saskatchewan River with its great length, and two branches, would seem to be a mighty waterway on a map of the Prairie Provinces.

Bruce Peel

The Great North-West

"Well, boy," he said, "this is the great North-West!"
There was a note in my father's voice which moved me.
Without being able to analyse my reaction, I was aware
that . . . he was proud of it, proud to be a part of it. I
responded to this ring of triumph; I too felt proud to be a
part of this great North-West. . . .

James M. Minifie

Winter Morning

When Earth puts on her ermine wrap
And holds white diamonds in her lap.

Edna Jaques

The Elevator

The elevators became so characteristic a feature of the landscape that the fact that they were not indigenous to it became lost in their very familiarity.

Jean Swanson

Prairie Sod

The plow cut through the new sod with a soft tearing
sound. An even width of earth curled away, to fall upside
down in a straight brown ribbon. Each succeeding round,
those ribbons fell precisely into the trench the plow had
left the round before. For the first time I understood the
difference between grassland and crop fields!

Nell Parsons

Prairie Fall

Woods still are candle-lit
by golden ash boughs
while forest aisles
are spread with royal garnet,
topaz and ruby leaves. Rich rumors
of ripening chokecherries scent
the air — silence is violated
only by a whisper of leaf fall,
swish of broad wings
and thrum of migrant cranes
over the coulee hills.

Mildred A. Rose

Welcome Rain

There were showers and torrents, the drought had broken, O, thank heaven, it *can* rain! And the scorched earth drank deep. Our prairie had not betrayed us.

Ethel Kirk Grayson

Northern Twilight

In that northern latitude twilight is incredibly long.
Though the whole vast sky might have been, and indeed
most surely was, cloudless throughout the long day, there
seemed always to be far-off clouds in a sort of shadowy
unreality, above the setting sun.

Nell Parsons

Prairie Hills

Plains, valleys, hills — I love them all. But especially the hills, the open hills, where the upward-sweeping wind gives a buoyancy to our cumbersome bodies and wings to our souls.

R. D. Symons

Song at Sunrise

Hail to thee, beautiful, mighty, and golden!
Rise in thy splendor and gladden the earth;
Banish the darkness, all good things embolden;
Shine, O life-giver, that joy may have birth.

Sister Maura

24

Snow Shadows

The tree shadows are blue. If you look at the cobalt sky
of a winter's day, then quickly back to a large patch of
shadow, that patch appears grey. But concentrate on that
shadow and you know it is blue, but quite a different
blue from the sky, more indigo . . . The warmer the
weather, the stronger these colors are.

R. D. Symons

Evening

And down on tiptoe came the gradual night,
A gentle twilight first, with silver wings,
And still from out the darkening infinite
Came shadowy forms, like day's imaginings.

Charles Sangster

Accomplishment

There was a great pride in my heart, when I saw the cultivation of our farm increasing year by year. We had taken fields of grass and turned them into fields of grain. We had brought the seed and soil together. . . .

Nellie McClung

Guardians

High over prairie towns
in storm or fairest weather,
red beacons to the wanderer
grain elevators tower —
tall sentinels of the plains.

Mildred A. Rose

Old Timer

He loves his land, the flat unbroken fields
Reaching away to meet the sky's blue rim,
This is his homestead . . . here he got his start,
The well, the pond, the barns, are part of him.
All his young strength he gave with lavish hand
To make a home in this new virgin land.

Edna Jaques

The Song My Paddle Sings

My paddle will lull you into rest,
O! drowsy wind of the drowsy west,
Sleep, sleep,
By your mountain steep,
Or down where the prairie grasses sweep!
Now fold in slumber your laggard wings,
For soft is the song my paddle sings.

E. Pauline Johnson
Tekahionwake

Prairie Gold

No mine is rich as these broad fields alive
With harvestry; no mineral as rare
As this red furrow ore which soon will pour
Down iron ways to glut great ports and drive
Across three seas to half the world and more
With summer's wealth and nature's elixir.

R. E. Rashley

Winter Morning

A morning crisp as watered silk,
With blankets of new fallen snow,
Tucking the little houses in,
For fear their naked feet will show,
The trees and shrubs are beautiful,
Wrapped in their coats of carded wool.

Edna Jaques

Letter Home

Replying to an English mother who wrote asking how she could bear living in Saskatchewan the author wrote: "This rich black soil forever and ever will be our own one day . . . All things one strives in a lifetime for in England are here all the time — fresh air, utter quiet, blue skies, trees, wild flowers, birds, animals, also garden space and a house . . . without a key for any door!"

A. E. M. Hewlett

Golden Things

A field of golden ripened wheat
Basking in waves of harvest heat,
When earth and sky and air are one,
Holding the radiance of the sun.

Edna Jaques

The Cloud-Burst

Down comes the rain in a cloud-burst, forming a wall in
front of them where they sit in the sheltering cove in
which all the fragrance of the meadow is concentrated.
Flashes of lightning break on the slough like bomb-shells;
rattling thunder dances and springs.

Frederick Philip Grove

Another Season

In an air-conditioned tractor cab
the past leans hard
on Old Jim's shoulders —
Other springs long ago,
yesterday's gulls in clouds
of morning joy in treasures
in the soft turned earth.
Horses strain in harnesses,
till the land and sow the seed —
The land, the land, always the land.

Mildred A. Rose

The Elevator

At convenient points along the branch lines . . . grain
elevators were erected to receive the bounty of the land

Jean Swanson

Autumn

Autumn is an old brave, loping along
in beaded moccasins.
The mischievous winds
are tearing down his painted teepee;
but he is headed South,
long braids flying,
and the sun glinting on his gaudy
head feathers.

Margot Osborn

Fulfillment

Listen, in the twilight
When winds sink to a sigh;
To murmurs of wealth from golden fields
Where precious wheat stands high.

The settler felt the promise,
Huddled beneath his tattered tarp,
Hearing siren wind-music
Strummed upon a sagebrush harp.

Nell Parsons

Just One More

He reversed the plow for another furrow;
and once he was committed to more than one round,
he stayed with the work till it was too dark to see.
He was here to conquer. Conquer he would! Before long
he had opened ten furrows; the sun was down; and
still he went on . . .

Frederick Philip Grove

I Love New Things

I love the newness of an April day,
Spring in the air . . . and summer on the way,
A quiet meadow where a nuthatch sings,
Above the shining lustre of new things.

Edna Jaques

The Fairyland

Coming home we drove into a fairyland. Low sun threw
shafts of light across snowy stubble; rows of golden stalks
stiff beside hollows where snow lay thick . . . sky above
blue, paling to faintest grey on the horizon through wisps
of purple cloud. In the northeast a full moon rose, while
to the south, its yellow disc hardly glowing, the sun
slowly sank.

A. E. M. Hewlett

The Wind Our Enemy

Horses were strong so strong men might love them,
Sides groomed to copper burning the sun,
Wind tangling wild manes, dust circling wild hoofs,
Turn the colts loose! Watch the two-year-olds run!

Anne Marriott

Grit and Granite

It takes patience and vigilance, the power to persist and the power to endure. It takes grit in the people to match the granite in the climate. They hang on, they grope for firmness, and sometimes they win.

Carlyle King

Hymn To The Forest

Ere man learned to raise a temple
With lofty vaulted dome,
In the darkling wood he knelt,
God's majesty to own.
Here a verdant roof was fashioned
From the naked ground,
And His breath among the treetops
Made mystic music sound.

Marietta Macdonald Silver

Letter Home

I love every bit of Canada already, the dear flat prairie, vaster and somehow bigger in all senses than we even imagined in the "Old Country".

A. E. M. Hewlett

Where the town lies

High above the prairie, platter-flat,
the wind wings on, bereft and wild its lonely song.
It ridges drifts and licks their ripples off; it smoothens
crests, piles snow against fences . . . Light glows each
evening where the town lies; a hiving sound is there, with
now and then some sound distinct and separate in the
night: a shout, a woman's laugh. Clear — truant sounds.

W. O. Mitchell

The Cry of the Loon

Far off the lonely crying of a loon
Echoes among the branches overhead,
Like an old woman wailing for her dead.

Edna Jaques

Prairie Bred

I'm lonesome for the old trails
That wound across the plain,
The willows by the coulee's rim
That swish against the rain;

Edna Jaques

Evening Stillness

The dusk was a magic time of day, so still that something seemed to reach inside you.

Nell Parsons

Take Time

Take time to really see a row
Of evergreens against the snow,
With slate-blue shadows by the gate
Like pictures on a Chinese plate;

Edna Jaques

October

You can see October
Like a carpet laid
Over all the little fields
Lovely as brocade.

Edna Jaques

Horizontal World

Not that there's easy beauty on the plains —
You catch it only from the earth and sky;
And then by living there, not for a day,
Or months, but years. In time, even the snow
In winter takes its hold on you, till there
Is no place else a man can live and feel
On terms with living. Horizontal worlds,
Somehow, catch all the height and breadth of sky.

Thomas Saunders

Landscape Locations

5 Near Clavet, **7** Near St. Louis, **9** Prongua District, **11** Near Biggar, **13** Osler, **15** Rosthern, **17** Qu'Appelle Valley, **19** North of Swift Current, **21** Lac la Ronge, **23** Saskatchewan Landing, **25** Brock, **27** Meadow Lake, **29** Waskesiu Lake, **31** Red Deer Hill, **33** Marquis, **35** Punnichy, **37** Pike Lake, **39** Balgonie, **41** Blucher, **43** Red Deer Hill, **45** Near Prince Albert, **47** Yorkton, **49** Davis, **51** Perdue, **53** Buffalo Pound Lake, **55** Saskatchewan Landing, **57** Near Saskatoon, **59** Cypress Hills Provincial Park, **61** Ridpath, **63** West of Nokomis, **65** Elstow, **67** Northern Saskatchewan Parkland, **69** Leader, **71** Looking to Valparaiso, **73** Northern Saskatchewan, **75** Maple Creek, **77** Potash mine reflections, rural Saskatoon, **79** Northern Boreal forest land, Northern Saskatchewan, **81** Qu'Appelle Valley, **83** Davidson.

Quotation Sources and Credits

The following sources are listed in the order in which they appear in the book. We gratefully acknowledge the permission granted by publishers and authors to reprint certain selections. Specific permissions are indicated with the appropriate quotation sources. Every effort has been made to obtain permission from holders of copyright. If omissions have occurred, Western Producer Prairie Books will be pleased to make adjustment upon notification from the copyright holder.

4 from **Who Has Seen the Wind** by W. O. Mitchell, published by Macmillan in 1947, page 3. Reprinted by permission of Macmillan of Canada.

6 from **Steamboats on the Saskatchewan** by Bruce Peel, published by Western Producer Prairie Books in 1972, page 1.

8 from **Homesteader: A Prairie Boyhood Recalled** by James M. Minifie, published by Macmillan in 1972, page 29. Reprinted by permission of Macmillan of Canada.

10 from "Winter Morning" in **The Best of Edna Jaques** by Edna Jaques, published by Western Producer Prairie Books in 1974.

12 from **Sky Painter** by Jean Swanson, published by Western Producer Prairie Books in 1973, page 17.

14 from **Upon a Sagebrush Harp** by Nell Wilson Parsons, published by Western Producer Prairie Books in 1969, page 18.

16 from "Prairie Fall" by Mildred A. Rose, Regina, Saskatchewan. Reprinted with Ms. Rose's permission.

18   from **Unbind the Sheaves** by Ethel Kirk Grayson, printed by Modern Press, Saskatoon, in 1964, page 122.
Reprinted with Mrs. Grayson's permission.

20   from **Upon a Sagebrush Harp** by Nell Wilson Parsons, published by Western Producer Prairie Books in 1969, page 22.

22   from **Silton Seasons: from the Diary of a Countryman** by R. D. Symons, published by Doubleday & Company Inc. in 1975, page 42. Copyright © 1975 by Hope Symons.
Reprinted by permission of Doubleday & Company Inc.

24   from "Deidre's Song at Sunrise" in **Rhyme and Rhythm** by Sister Maura, published by Ryerson Press in 1932.

26   from **Silton Seasons: from the Diary of a Countryman** by R. D. Symons, published by Doubleday & Company Inc. in 1975, page 144. Copyright © 1975 by Hope Symons.
Reprinted by permission of Doubleday & Company Inc.

28   from "Evening" by Charles Sangster in **Canadian Poetry in English,** published by Ryerson Press in 1954.

30   from **Our Nell: A Scrapbook Biography of Nellie L. McClung** by Candace Savage, published by Western Producer Prairie Books in 1979, page 11.

32   from "Guardians" by Mildred A. Rose, Regina, Saskatchewan.
Reprinted with Ms. Rose's permission.

34   from "Old Timer" in **Prairie Born, Prairie Bred** by Edna Jaques, published by Western Producer Prairie Books in 1979.

36   from "The Song My Paddle Sings" in **Flint and Feather** by E. Pauline Johnson.
Copyright © 1931 Hodder & Stoughton Canada Ltd.
Reprinted with the permission of Hodder & Stoughton Canada.

38   from "Prairie Gold" in **Voyageur and Other Poems** by R. E. Rashley, published by Ryerson Press in 1946.
Reprinted with Mrs. Rashley's permission.

40   from "Winter Morning" in **The Best of Edna Jaques** by Edna Jaques, published by Western Producer Prairie Books in 1974.

42   from **A Too Short Yesterday** by A. E. M. Hewlett, published by Golden Harvest Book Service (Western Producer Prairie Books) in 1970, page 95.

44   from "Golden Things" in **The Best of Edna Jaques** by Edna Jaques, published by Western Producer Prairie Books in 1974.

46   from **Settlers of the Marsh** by Frederick Philip Grove, published by Ryerson Press in 1925, page 147.

48   from "Another Season" by Mildred A. Rose, Regina, Saskatchewan.
Reprinted with Ms. Rose's permission.

50   from **Sky Painter** by Jean Swanson, published by Western Producer Prairie Books in 1973, page 17.

52   from "Autumn" in **Frosty Moon and Other Poems** by Margot Osborn, published by Ryerson Press in 1946.

54   from **Upon a Sagebrush Harp** by Nell Wilson Parsons, published by Western Producer Prairie Books in 1969.

56   from **The Fruits of the Earth** by Frederick Philip Grove, published by J. M. Dent & Sons in 1933, page 15. Reprinted with the permission of J. M. Dent & Sons (Canada) Ltd.

58   from "I Love New Things" in **The Best of Edna Jaques** by Edna Jaques, published by Western Producer Prairie Books in 1974.

60   from **A Too Short Yesterday** by A. E. M. Hewlett, published by Golden Harvest Book Service (Western Producer Prairie Books) in 1970, page 60.

62   from **The Wind Our Enemy** by Anne Marriott, published by Ryerson Press in 1939, page 3. By permission of the author, Anne Marriott McLellan.

64   from **Far Horizons, Man Alone** by Carlyle King, published by Western Producer Prairie Books in 1974, page 13. Reprinted with the author's permission.

66   from "Hymn to the Forest" in **Sandy and Other Poems** by Marietta Macdonald Silver, printed by Black Printing Co. Ltd., 1978. Reprinted with Mrs. Silver's permission.

68   from **A Too Short Yesterday** by A. E. M. Hewlett, published by Golden Harvest Book Service (Western Producer Prairie Books) in 1970, page 12.

70   from **Who Has Seen the Wind** by W. O. Mitchell, published by Macmillan of Canada in 1947, page 295. Reprinted by permission of Macmillan of Canada.

72   from "Fall Leaves" in **Prairie Born, Prairie Bred** by Edna Jaques, published by Western Producer Prairie Books in 1979.

74   from "Prairie Born" in **Prairie Born, Prairie Bred** by Edna Jaques, published by Western Producer Prairie Books in 1979.

76   from **Upon A Sagebrush Harp** by Nell Wilson Parsons, published by Western Producer Prairie Books in 1969, page 76.

78   from "Take Time" in **Prairie Born, Prairie Bred** by Edna Jaques, published by Western Producer Prairie Books in 1979.

80   from "October" in **Prairie Born, Prairie Bred** by Edna Jaques, published by Western Producer Prairie Books in 1979.

82   from **Horizontal World** by Thomas Saunders, published by Ryerson Press in 1951, page 1.